Special Delivery

Donna Gray,
This was my greatest eight week headache, yours is yet to come; but real soon.
Tenn Smoot

Since the beginning of time or as far back as anyone can recall, the Royal Order of the Stork has held the duty of delivering all the babies in the world. Without fail they had never missed a delivery or had trouble meeting their quota, until one day a very special egg came into their possession. This egg was like no other, for it was the only one of its kind left in the world. It was a Doe-Doe egg. The storks were baffled because they did not know what to do. There were no other Doe-Does they could deliver the egg to. This egg was truly an orphan.

After a few days passed, the egg hatched. It was a boy. The storks all gathered because they had never seen a baby Doe-Doe. They were so rare that no living stork could ever recall even hearing about one so, this was truly a treat. He was extremely cute, he had red feathers with an orange beak and legs but, there was just something about his eyes that indeed made him special. Everyone could see he was destined to do great things since he was the last of the Doe-Doe birds.

Greybeard, the oldest and wisest stork, took it upon himself to raise the hatchling as one of his own. Greybeard named him Donnie. As Donnie grew, he watched the storks in their daily task of delivering the babies. The older he became the more he wanted to deliver the babies. His desire became the one thing he wanted more than anything else. But as he grew, Greybeard noticed that the older Donnie became, the more apparent it was that Donnie had Average Doe-Doe Disorder. Commonly known as A.D.D., this was a common condition for Doe-Does, because of this and the fact that Doe-Does cannot fly, Donnie would never be allowed to deliver any babies.

Everything was going great for the storks until one day the storks had to deliver a baby chicken to Henrietta Hen. But, when the delivery was made they did not know that Henrietta was sick with the bird flu, so the delivery bird became ill too. When he returned to headquarters, he unknowingly gave the flu to the rest of the storks. So one by one, the storks became ill until the entire fleet was infected with the flu. Due to the outbreak Greybeard was forced to ground the fleet. This was terrible for the storks because they would not be able to deliver any babies and that meant orders would pile up. They had to think of something quick to keep things going. Donnie offered to step in and take care of the deliveries but, to the storks this was out of the question. After a few days had past, the deliveries were really piling up so despite of their better judgment, the storks knew they had to give Donnie his chance to deliver the eggs.

Ace Longfeather was a tall stork, with an athletic build, trim and fit with a brash attitude to match. Anyone could see he was a top-notch delivery bird. Ace held the record for the most deliveries and fastest delivery time. To Donnie, he was the greatest delivery bird that ever lived. All the storks knew that if there was going to be any hope for Donnie to get the job done, it would be due to the guidance of Ace. Reluctantly, Ace agreed to help Donnie get ready. Donnie was so happy he could not wait to work with his hero. Donnie's dream was sure to come true now. But, there was much to do, so they had to get started right away. Ace cleared one of the flight hangers to get Donnie ready.

Ace went over flight instructions while Donnie sat patiently listening to every word. Even though it was hard for him to pay attention having A.D.D., Donnie tried his best not to let his mind wander. From take off to emergency landings, Ace covered everything he knew about flight. The more instructions they went over, the more confidence Donnie gained. All the storks knew Donnie had a problem with directions. Their plan was to get the headquarters as close to the delivery spot as possible, so Donnie would not have so far to go. Ace could tell Donnie was really trying but, the main problem still remained that Donnie was a Doe-Doe and Doe-Does cannot fly. Ace racked his brain coming up with ideas that might work to get Donnie around.

Out of all the ideas that Ace could come up with, they decided to try three and see which one would work best. His first idea was a rocket, because with Ace a fast delivery was a key issue. He wanted Donnie to be able to deliver as fast as he could. But, when Donnie tried to use the rocket, it was too heavy and uncontrollable.

Ace's second idea was a kite. This was a great idea, but wind played a big factor as to how well it actually worked, and the landings were just too rough for babies.

The third idea was balloons, although with this idea the wind was still a problem. They figured out Donnie could maneuver around using his arms and legs, and the landings were gentle enough for the babies. To get back up to the headquarters, all Donnie had to do was inflate more balloons and he would go up. This was indeed the way to go. So, they gave Donnie a basket with two eggs, one on top of the other and let him practice flying. After three or four hours, Donnie had flying down to a science. Donnie was so happy because all birds love to fly. Now that Donnie could fly, Greybeard let Donnie know he would be making his first delivery to the zoo.

Donnie was extremely excited about delivering to the zoo. Greybeard let him know that he had to deliver two eggs and one heavy load, which was a baby elephant. But, along with his instructions Greybeard gave a warning, you must watch out for the guard dogs Lonnie and Pip.

Lonnie and Pip had been working at the zoo for what seemed like forever. Lonnie was a large brute of a dog, but he was not very smart. Pip had a bad nervous disorder but an extremely keen sense of smell, he was faster than Lonnie and twice as mean which made him the more dangerous of the two. The storks had had many run-ins with these guard dogs in the past. The storks do not know why they try so hard to catch them but, Donnie needed to avoid them at all cost.

Donnie arrived at the zoo making a perfect landing. He was given a map by Greybeard, so he knew exactly where he was and felt confident he could get the job done. He looked around and could see no sign of Lonnie and Pip. While on his way to deliver the first egg, he accidentally stepped in a puddle of water. Donnie paid no attention to the tracks he was leaving, as he made his way to Abigail Alligator, which is where the first egg needed to go. A few minutes later Pip came by, saw the tracks left behind by Donnie and knew someone was in the zoo.

Pip immediately let Lonnie know someone was in the zoo. Lonnie and Pip decided they would set a trap to catch Donnie. Pip, being the smarter of the two, could tell by the direction of the tracks which way he was going and how far Donnie had gone. After thinking about it long and hard, they decided to set up an ambush which meant they would simply wait in the bushes until Donnie walked by, then jump out and surprise him.

Just like Pip figured, it was only a short amount of time before Donnie came by. When Donnie reached the right spot, Pip and Lonnie sprang the trap. To look at Donnie you would not think he could run that fast but, Lonnie and Pip soon found that he was faster than they were. Donnie took off like a rocket running through the zoo. Even he did not know he could run that fast. He ran up one path and down another. When Donnie finally slowed down to look back, he noticed the dogs were nowhere in sight. He had gotten away from Lonnie and Pip.

Unfortunately for Donnie, he soon discovered that he was lost. He tried to locate where he was by using Greybeard's map but, the excitement of being chased and his A.D.D. just was not letting him concentrate. Donnie decided to ask for directions. The closest animal Donnie could find was Zendo the panda. Donnie explained to Zendo that he was lost and needed directions to Abigail Alligator.

Zendo could not understand a word Donnie said. Donnie did not know Zendo was a foreign exchange animal from China. He did not speak English and mistakenly thought Donnie was looking for Bo-Bo the gorilla and pointed Donnie in the wrong direction.

Donnie climbed into Bo-Bo's cage, looked around and did not see anyone. Bo-Bo saw Donnie and immediately mistook him for a prowler. For a very large and muscular animal, Bo-Bo was quite sneaky, he crept up behind Donnie and before Donnie even knew he was there, Bo-Bo had him.

Bo-Bo had a nasty attitude and did not like anyone in his cage. Bo-Bo worked Donnie over good, throwing him from one side of the cage to the other. He jumped on him, swung him around, and threw him into the wall. After pounding on Donnie for quite some time, Bo-Bo noticed the basket of eggs. He loved babies. Bo-Bo knew he had made a mistake and apologized to Donnie. Just then Lonnie and Pip walked by, Lonnie saw Donnie in the cage because he had gotten away before Lonnie became furious.

Lonnie and Pip ran into the cage after Donnie. With the basket of eggs in hand, Donnie took off running. Around the cage he went faster and faster, jumping over everything in his path. Bo-Bo was stunned watching the dogs chase after him. Pip tried to cut Donnie off, but there was just no catching the doe-doe bird. Suddenly, Bo-Bo told Donnie to jump the wall. He was so tired, he did not think he could make it but, he had to try. Donnie made one more lap, got a big running start and jumped as hard as he could. He barely made it to the top of the wall with the dogs on his heels and with a sigh of relief he was out of the cage.

Bo-Bo was enraged. He could not believe anyone would be after someone delivering babies. Tired from chasing Donnie, Lonnie and Pip did not have the energy to get away from Bo-Bo. He grabbed the dogs and told Donnie to take as much time as needed to finish making his deliveries. Donnie was exhausted, so he gladly thanked Bo-Bo for his help.

When Donnie turned to continue his task, he saw Penny Penguin standing on her ice block. Even though this was not the first delivery on his list, Donnie knew the second egg belonged to her. When Donnie gave Penny her egg, she gave him directions to Abigail Alligator.

Donnie followed Penny's directions and soon found himself at the alligator tank. Abigail was so happy to see him and Donnie was overjoyed the eggs were delivered. Now all he had to do was deliver the heavy load.

Donnie inflated some balloons and headed back up to headquarters. The storks were happy that Donnie was almost finished. He had just one more delivery. Tubby the baby elephant was much too heavy for balloons, so the stork gathered all the rope they could find and lowered Tubby down. Donnie worked and worked carrying the baby elephant. It seemed like the more he carried it, the heavier it became. After lugging the elephant around for about an hour, Donnie had only gone thirty feet and needed a break.

Donnie thought he would never get finished. He was much too tired to carry Tubby any farther, so he decided to drag Tubby the rest of the way. Tubby's mom Sue, saw Donnie coming and met him halfway. She was so happy that she picked Tubby up and made her way home.

Donnie never knew delivering babies could be so difficult but, he was really proud that he got the job done. When Donnie returned to headquarters, Greybeard let him know he had done well and would be allowed to deliver from now on. Donnie was famous among the storks because he was the Doe-Doe that saved the day!